PRIMARY 1 & 2

AF856680

Tips and Tricks for Creative Writing

Writing with Friends at the Playground

WS Education

NEW JERSEY • LONDON • SINGAPORE • BEIJING • SHANGHAI • TAIPEI • CHENNAI

Published by

WS Education, an imprint of
World Scientific Publishing Co. Pte. Ltd.
5 Toh Tuck Link, Singapore 596224
USA office: 27 Warren Street, Suite 401-402, Hackensack, NJ 07601
UK office: 57 Shelton Street, Covent Garden, London WC2H 9HE

National Library Board, Singapore Cataloguing in Publication Data
Name(s): Ong, Matthew. | Ooi, Mark, author. | Ong, Jean, author. | Bay, Alan, illustrator.
Title: Writing with friends at the playground. Primary 1 & 2 / by Matthew Ong, Mark Ooi, Jean Ong ; illustrated by Alan Bay.
Other Title(s): Tips and tricks for creative writing.
Description: Singapore : WS Education, [2025]
Identifier(s): ISBN 978-981-98-1117-5 (paperback)
Subject(s): LCSH: English language--Composition and exercises--Study and teaching (Primary)--Juvenile literature. | Creative writing (Primary education)--Juvenile literature.
Classification: DDC 372.623--dc23

British Library Cataloguing-in-Publication Data
A catalogue record for this book is available from the British Library.

Printed in Malaysia

Contents

Introduction

Dear Reader,

Do you know that you have a *wonderful gift*? No, it's not just being fast or smart or beautiful.

You are able to create and write your own stories! Just let your thoughts and imagination run wild and write them down! When students sit in a class and are asked to write a story, many freeze. They don't know what to do. It's difficult for a number of reasons. They may ask or think:

- What do I write about? I don't know how to start.
- I have some ideas, but I don't know how to write about them.
- My English is bad. I don't want you to think badly of me.
- I don't know exactly what you (the teacher/reader) really want.

However, *everyone* has wonderful ideas. Let's imagine for a second. Look at this shape below, what do you see? If you asked different people that same question, you would get many different answers.

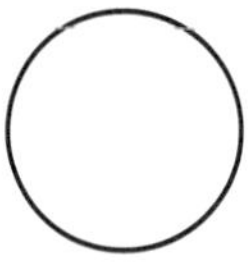

Could it be a circle? Perhaps a ball? An egg missing a yolk? There are so many things that it could represent.

As a writer, you have control over how you tell the story. You can change what the readers imagine in their own minds as they read your story. Let's go back to the shape above. If you decided to add something to it, you could guide your reader into imagining it as the sun!

When we write stories, we might feel that it's too difficult. We might even think that we just don't have the ability or skill that others might have. However, this is **not** true and that's the reason for this book.

We want you to know that of the 8.2 billion people in the world, there is just one of you. And that makes you ***special***. It makes ***your*** ideas special. So, let's celebrate that!

Before we get started, let me introduce you to three special friends who will be joining us on this journey of discovery and learning. Each of them has wonderful ideas, hopes and dreams.

Monkey loves to share his ideas. He is always curious to learn new things!

Elephant remembers everything. You can count on him! He loves sharing what he has learnt to help others learn new things.

Parrot loves nothing more than to chirp and sing, often with delightful rhyme!

You could say that they were born with great gifts and are naturally good at what they do. But that would not be entirely true! It has taken time for Monkey to share and express himself confidently. It has taken effort for Elephant to build up his memory strength in the writing gym. It's taken months for Parrot to learn to sing so confidently.

Right now, however, they are keen on learning how to become better writers. If you've opened this book, I'm sure you are too. So, let's get started!

WAIT! I forgot to mention Skunk! Look out for Weasel too! They are up to no good.

Skunk is sneaky. He creeps around trying to find out what Monkey and friends are learning. Watch out for him trying to throw them off course!

Weasel is Skunk's trusted friend. They want to be better than the other animals — at all costs!

Yours truly,
Coach

CHAPTER 1 My Greatest Experiences

Details and order can bring great wonder!
If you ever feel stuck, focus on your feelings. How did you feel during that moment? Feelings are like the colours in a painting. They help others to understand or 'see' your story more clearly!
Excellent advice, everyone! Now that we've got some ideas flowing, who's ready to share their greatest experience with us?
Me, me, me! I'll go first! I remember the time I found a hidden waterfall in the jungle!
Well, I was swinging through the trees when I heard the sound of rushing water. I followed the sound and pushed through some big leaves...
That sounds amazing, Monkey! What did you feel when you saw the waterfall?
I felt so amazed and happy and proud! It felt like I had found something really special, just for me!
Found a treasure, found a sight, made you feel just right! Tell us more, my friend. How did it end?
Hmm... I felt so cosy that I wanted to stay there forever, but I knew I had to get back home before dark.
Thank you, Monkey! That was a fantastic example of your greatest experience.
Remember that a personal recount is a story that is told through your eyes. It is also something that you have experienced yourself.
Maybe someone could tell us about a time they helped someone, or learned something new?
New friends, new things. Oh, what joy they bring! Share your tale, don't be shy, let your words fly high!
I'm glad I could share my story! Don't worry about getting it perfect. Just tell us what happened, how you felt and why it was special to you!
Every story is special, and we're excited to hear yours. We will start with some fun drawing activities!
I will need you to draw your favourite memory. Are you ready?

Inspiration

My Greatest Experiences

Draw a picture of your greatest experience.

What is your favourite part of this experience? How did you feel about it?

Well done! It was wonderful to learn about your favourite memory through the picture you drew!
With that great experience waiting to be told...
Ooh, ooh, what's next?
I'm glad to see you so excited, Monkey! Do you know what the main parts of a story are?
Patience, Monkey! Give him some space to talk.
The experience?
Yes, Monkey, but Coach is talking about the main parts of it! Listen carefully.
Yes, thank you, Elephant! When we write a story, we have the things that happen, but we also need to think about the characters that appear, the setting (place) the story takes place in...
And also the problem the main character faces and how they overcome it!
Characters and settings, a great wonder! Oh, what a delight! They make your story shine so bright!
I think she used the same song earlier...
Did someone say something?
I don't think so but it's starting to smell strange around here...
Yes, I smell it too!
I think they're talking about you, Skunk!
Very funny, stop being looney. They can't see us when we're hidden in these pages!
Alright, I think the smell is gone. Let's look more closely at the characters of our story...

Key Idea

PERSONAL RECOUNT: *Telling a story of something that you have experienced.*

Personal recounts are a way for the writer to share his/her experiences with someone else.

In the past, people had to write letters to share things over long distances, such as with friends who lived in faraway places.

Today, we can share something with someone on the other side of the planet with our computers or mobile phones.

People share their personal recounts very often on computers today!

For this personal recount, we will focus on the characters and setting.

Characters

Imagine that you are writing a story. You are the main character.

Who else appears in your story?
How can you describe them to your reader?

How do these other characters look like?

Describe their personality.
Are they kind, fierce, patient, impatient or honest?

Story Parts

Characters

Answer these guiding questions, then draw two of the characters who appear in your greatest experience.

Question for your characters	Answer
What is their hairstyle? Do they have long or short hair?	
What are they wearing?	
What are they doing?	
How do they feel?	

Wonderful! It was great to learn more about your story. Now, we understand who appears in your personal recount, where the story happens and what made it a special experience for you.
Yes, yes, what's next?
With that wonderful story waiting to be written...
What's next? What's next?
Monkey! So impatient and excited as usual...
I'm glad to see you so excited, Monkey! Now that we have the main parts of your story...
The characters? The setting?
Yes, Monkey, we have those things. I think we can now write our very own personal recount!
When we write a story, we need to remember that they are like puzzles. As we plan a story, we begin to see where the characters, settings, problem and solution fit together!
It's like putting jigsaw parts together. I love jigsaw puzzles.
What do you think might happen if we take away a character from a story?
Um... you won't have a story then?
Oh wow... yes, I think you're right, Weasel. Characters are like the pillars in a building. Would you say I'm an important character in the jungle, Weasel?
Absolutely! There's no one like you, Skunk. Who else would make the place stink?
Why you!?
Now, we need to make sure that our personal recount is written in the same order of what we experienced. Take a look at these helpful worksheets to do this!

Story Parts

Monkey's Story – How It Begins

I had just bathed in the river. My brown fur shimmered in the sunlight as I swung between trees. My large, curious eyes always seemed to sparkle with excitement. My long, curly tail helped me to balance myself. I was laughing as I swung around, thinking about my next adventure.

Your turn! Draw a picture of how your story begins.

Describe what is happening in the picture in two or three sentences.

Story Parts

Monkey's Story – The Middle

One afternoon, I was swinging through the jungle. Suddenly, I noticed a narrow, winding path that I had never seen before. My heart started beating extremely quickly. I was curious where the path would lead. I looked around to check for danger. I decided to follow the path. My tail was twitching with excitement! The air grew cooler as I walked towards a hidden cave. It was mysterious because its entrance was covered in thick vines and moss.

Your turn! Draw a picture of what happens in the middle of your story.

Describe what is happening in the picture in two or three sentences.

Story Parts

Monkey's Story – The End

Inside the cave, my eyes widened in amazement. The walls glowed with sparkling gems of every colour. The gems were reflecting light all over the walls of the cave. I gently touched one. It felt cold and smooth. I laughed and smiled because I had found something special. I made sure I remembered the location of the cave. I left the cave to return home to bring a bag. I needed something to carry the gemstones.

Your turn! Draw a picture of what happens in the end of your story.

Describe what is happening in the picture in two or three sentences.

Yippee, hooray! We are so close now, I can feel it!
Now that we have everything about your experience wonderfully drawn out and written...
What's next? What's next?
Monkey, let Coach talk!
Now that we have everything we need, we just need to combine all of it... So your readers can read your wonderful story at one go!

I love solving difficult puzzles...
Especially when it's all done!

My Greatest Experience

Write all your colourful sentences here to create a story of your greatest experience.

Introduction Who are your characters? Where is the story taking place?	
Middle What happened to your main character? What was the problem? How was it solved	
End What happened in the end?	

Monkey is brave and kind,
he never leaves his friends behind.
All the friends know that they can depend
on each other until they reach the end.

Elephant enjoys his day.
He finds all his fun along the way.
His greatest moments, so full of joy,
are stories everyone will enjoy.

Parrot sings wonderful songs
with perfect tone that never goes wrong.
There's always a special rhyme
for friends singing all the time.

CHAPTER 2

My Wonderful Story

Those are all great ideas! The setting can be anywhere you can imagine — underwater, in the zoo or even in your home. The setting helps make your story more exciting. It can also change how your characters act. For example, how would you feel in a cold, snowy place?
Brrr! I'd be so cold and want a jacket!
I'd probably stay close to a fire to stay warm.
Did you see that? The setting affects what your characters do and how they feel. Today, when you think of your story, remember to make your setting fun and interesting.
It helps the readers imagine where everything happens. What kind of story would you tell if it happened on a pirate ship?
I'd be swinging on ropes, looking for treasure!
I'd be sitting on the captain's shoulder, singing pirate songs!
I'd help steer the ship through big waves and storms!
And that's how the setting makes your story come alive! It's not just where the story happens, but also how the characters feel and what they do. First, let's have some fun thinking about our story ideas!

Inspiration

My Wonderful Story

Draw a picture of your wonderful story.

What is your favourite part of this story?

Wow! It was fantastic to learn about your wonderful story through your drawing!
Yay, what's next?
I'm going to write it! What's next?
With that wonderful story waiting to be written...
Always so excited, Monkey! Let Coach speak!
Catch your breath, Monkey! Let's do it step by step. Do you know what are the key parts of a story?
The experience?
Yes, but Coach is talking about the parts of it! That means the characters that appear, the setting the story takes place in... And also the problem the characters face and how they solve it!
When we write a story, we cannot just focus on what happens... We need to think about the setting too! The place where the story happens.
Characters and settings, a great wonder! Oh, what a delight! They make your story shine so bright!
Today, let's look more closely at the setting of our story...

Key Idea

PERSONAL NARRATIVE: *Telling a story of something that you have experienced.*

Personal narratives are a way for the writer to share his/her experiences with someone else. These stories are written about something that was special to the writer. The writer usually talks about facing a problem and how he/she overcame it!

As this is a personal narrative, you are the main character. Let's take a look at the setting and where the story is taking place.

Setting

Where is the story taking place? This is important because your reader needs to know where your story happens. It is very different for a sleepover to happen at your home or on the slope of a volcano!

Story Parts

Setting

Answer these guiding questions, then draw the setting you have described.

Imagine that you are in a magical forest...

Question	Answer
What kind of trees and plants are there? Are they tall or short? Colourful?	
What kind of animals do you see?	
How do you feel in the forest? Are you safe or in danger? Is it cold or hot?	
What is one special thing you see in the forest?	

Story Parts

Setting

Answer these guiding questions, then draw the setting you have described.

Imagine that you are in school...

Question	Answer
What do you see and hear?	
What do you smell and taste?	
What time of the day is it? What is the weather like?	
What is one special thing that stands out to you?	

Super! Now that we know more about settings, let's take this one step further.
What's next? It's time to write your wonderful story!
Yes, yes, what's next?
Yippee! I've been waiting all day for this!
Monkey... I'm expecting a wonderful story!
Next, we will write our story in three parts. We will have the beginning, middle and end! This should make it easier for you to think about your story in different scenes.
I remember doing this in the previous chapter... I'm sure I can do it again. I'm sure I can do it even better than before!
Yes, Monkey, that was a lovely story you wrote. We're looking forward to this story too!
Thank you, Elephant! Monkey, remember that looking at your drawing of your story and your drawing of the setting can help you with your story!
For some help in writing the story in three parts... Take a look at Monkey's story and use these helpful worksheets to write one of your own! Remember to talk about the setting using what we've already learnt!

Story Parts

Monkey's Story – How It Begins

One sunny morning, I was swinging on vines through the jungle. The birds were chirping a wonderful song. The leaves and branches moved in the wind. It looked like they were waving at me. I set off on an adventure with some water and bananas. I had heard whispers of a secret waterfall deep within the jungle. No one had ever found it before. Filled with excitement, I decided that today would be the day I discovered the hidden treasure. I was determined to follow every clue and explore every path until I found it.

Your turn! Draw a picture of how your story begins.

Describe what is happening in the picture in two or three sentences.

Story Parts

Monkey's Story – The Middle

I tried my best to follow the distant sound of rushing water. *This must be the right way!* I thought, my heart pounding with excitement. Suddenly, the sound of rushing water grew louder. There was a problem. Giant boulders blocked the path ahead. I scratched my head. I had to figure out how to get past them. I climbed up the side of the rocks. I had to be careful as I climbed. It was a difficult climb. I almost fell off!

Your turn! Draw a picture of what happens in the middle of your story.

Describe what is happening in the picture in two or three sentences.

____

____

____

Story Parts

Monkey's Story – The End

I reached the top at last. I gasped in amazement. I was looking straight at the hidden waterfall. It was surrounded by bright flowers and lush greenery. The sunlight and water created tiny rainbows all around. I smiled and jumped into the water. I had finally found a secret spot no one else had ever seen! I loved the soothing sounds of the water. I felt so proud of this adventure. I couldn't wait to share this with my friends!

Your turn! Draw a picture of what happens in the end.

Describe what is happening in the picture in two or three sentences.

Yippee, hooray! We are so close now, I can feel it!
Now that we have everything about your experience wonderfully drawn out and written...
What's next? What's next?
Monkey! Let Coach talk!
Now that we have everything we need... We just need to combine all of it... So your readers can read your wonderful story at one go!

Hey there! What's your favourite story? Could you share it with me please?

My Greatest Experience

Write all your colourful sentences here to create a story of your greatest experience.

Introduction Who are your characters? Where is the story taking place?	
Middle What happened to your main character? What was the problem? How was it solved?	
End What happened in the end?	

In a forest, where many tall trees sway,
the flowers bloom and kids love to play.
Sunlight dances on leaves that are green.
It's the best place that I've ever seen.

Beautiful plants and flowers grow
by the river where the water flows.
This bright, big world is full of cheer.
A wonderful place where dreams come near.

CHAPTER 3

Hurray! It's My Story!

Inspiration

Can you think about a favourite memory?

Draw a picture of you in your favourite memory!

What was special about this memory?

Start with a thought, start with a scene, make it fun, make it keen!
That's one way to put it, Parrot! Remember, every story has characters, a setting, a problem and a solution. Getting lost must have been a difficult experience!
That sounds like a great story, Monkey! Start by telling us… Where were you? What were you doing before you got lost?
Remember to share your thoughts and feelings too! Were you scared, or did you feel like an explorer on an adventure?
Tell us the place, tell us the time, what did you see, what did you find, how did it feel, what was on your mind?
Okay, I'll start! I was playing in the trees, swinging from vine to vine. I wasn't paying attention… Suddenly, I realised I didn't know where I was. The trees looked different, and I couldn't hear any familiar sounds.
What happened? Did you fall?
A monkey falling from a tree? That's hilarious!
Don't be mean! Every animal has a 'superpower'. How would you like it if you lost your superpower?
You mean not being the smelliest creature on the planet? Are you making fun of me again?
Whoops! I didn't mean it like that!
Yes, it was a hard fall, but thankfully I landed on another small tree.
Sounds like you had a real problem then.
Ah! Every story needs a problem or a challenge. Great work, Monkey!
I'm not sure he wanted that problem to happen though!

Key Idea

PERSONAL NARRATIVE: *Telling a story of something that you have experienced.*

Personal narratives are a way for the writer to share his/her experiences with someone else. These stories are written about something that was special to the writer. The writer usually talks about facing a problem and how he/she overcame it.

As this is a personal narrative, you are the main character.

For this story, we will focus on the problem you faced and how it was solved.

Problem	What was the main problem you faced? Why was it a problem to you?
Solution	Who solved problem in the end? How was the problem solved? Did you learn anything from this experience?

Story Parts

Problem

Think about these questions below as you plan your story.

Question	Your thoughts
What caused the problem? Did someone cause the problem?	
What happened when things started to go wrong?	
How did you feel during this time? What did you see/hear/smell/feel?	
Did you learn anything from this experience?	

Draw what happened when you faced the problem.

Story Parts

Solution

Think about these questions below as you plan your story.

Question	Answer
How was the problem solved?	
Did it take a long time to solve the problem?	
Who solved the problem? How did he/she/they solve it?	
How did you feel after the problem was solved?	

Draw what happened when the problem was solved.

That sounds like a great story because it's something that's personal to you. Keep going and tell us what happened next!
I started to panic, but then I remembered that Elephant always says to stay calm. I looked for familiar things like the big tree I always swing past.
I climbed to the top of it and looked around until I saw my way home. I was so happy that I finally found my way home!
That's wonderful, Monkey! You did a great job telling us what happened, how you felt and how you solved the problem. That's what makes a personal narrative so interesting.
You used your memory to guide your story. Sharing those details helps others imagine what it was really like.
The way you described the setting and your emotions made it feel like we were right there with you. That's what makes your story wonderful.
Found the way, found the path, shared your journey, made us laugh!
Thank you, Monkey! That was a great example of a personal narrative. Now, who else would like to share their story? Remember, it doesn't have to be about getting lost. It could be about anything special or memorable that happened to you.
Think about a time when you learned something new, helped someone, or just had a lot of fun. Those moments make the best stories because they show who you are and what's important to you.
And don't forget to include the little details. They make your story come alive for your readers.
Yes, just start with the beginning, talk about the problem and then share how you solved the problem. If you can, share what you learnt too!

Story Parts

Monkey's Story – How It Begins

One bright morning, I was feeling extra adventurous. "I know this jungle extremely well," I said confidently. I did not want to swing along my usual path. I decided to explore a part of the jungle I had never been to before. I swung from tree to tree. Soon, the sounds of familiar animals faded away. I felt scared when I realised that I was lost. I tried to look for help, but no one else was there.

Your turn! Draw a picture of how your story begins.

Describe what is happening in the picture in two or three sentences.

Story Parts

Monkey's Story – The Middle

I tried to retrace my steps. However, every tree and vine looked the same. My heart started to race. *Maybe I took a wrong turn*, I thought nervously. I climbed higher up the tree. I hoped it would help me find my way home. However, the thick leaves made it hard to see anything. There were no familiar sounds around me. I began to worry that I would never return home. I did not want to be stuck here. I missed eating bananas on my favourite branch of my favourite tree.

Your turn! Draw a picture of what happens in the middle of your story.

Describe what is happening in the picture in two or three sentences.

Story Parts

Monkey's Story – The End

Suddenly, I heard a familiar sound. A group of parrots were singing in the distance! I followed the sound. After five minutes, I was in a familiar place. I swung down from the trees. I let out a deep sigh of relief and smiled. "I guess even the best adventurers can get lost sometimes," I laughed to myself. From that day on, I promised to stick to familiar paths. I did not want to get lost again.

Your turn! Draw a picture of what happens in the end.

Describe what is happening in the picture in two or three sentences.

Start, middle and end, that's the way. Let your story flow and sway!
Yeah! I did not worry about it being perfect… I just told it my own way!
There's just one more step to go, Monkey.
We're almost there! Combine the three parts of your story into one so that the reader can read it altogether!
Did I forget something?
Oh, yes! I almost forgot!
I'm so proud of you for telling your story, Monkey. Let's hear what our friends have to share next. Who's ready?

My Wonderful Story

Write all your colourful sentences here to create a story of your greatest experience.

Introduction Who are your characters? Where is the story taking place?	
Middle What happened to your main character? What was the problem? How was it solved?	
End What happened in the end?	

One day in the forest, Monkey lost his red hat.
He searched high and low, but only found a rat.
"Oh no! Where is it? I want it back fast!"
He looked in the trees and ran home at last.

Then Elephant said, "Let's think of a plan!
We'll ask Parrot too! Together, we can!"
And so they searched, not stopping to pout,
with friends all together, they'll find it, no doubt!

They looked in the river and under the leaves.
Day and night, they worked like bees.
Finally, in a bush, the hat was in sight!
They cheered and laughed. What a beautiful sight!

"Now I have my hat, thanks to my good friends!"
With smiles and joy, their adventure would soon end.
Problems may come up along your way.
Don't worry! Ask for help and you'll solve it today!

CHAPTER 4 Time to Rhyme

Wow... I think you just made a little rhyme. These animals are teaching us slowly with time!
I wonder what rhymes with pyjamas!
That's a great start, Parrot! Let's see if we can build a whole poem around that word. Maybe it could be about a fun day in pyjamas eating bananas.
Hmm... that sounds so silly, doesn't it? What if people don't take me seriously?
Silliness can be wonderful in poetry, Monkey. Poetry is all about expressing yourself. Sometimes, being silly is just what we need. In fact, Edward Lear wrote a whole book about nonsense!
Great! I like being silly! How about this: I climbed a tree, So that I could be free. But as I ate my bananas, I forgot I was still in my pyjamas!
That's a great rhyme, Monkey! You used your memory to create a fun image in our minds. Keep going!
And remember, you can add more lines to your poem. What happens after you eat the banana? Or after you climb to the top of the tree?
More rhymes, more fun, the poem's begun. Don't rest until it is done!
Your poem is coming along wonderfully, Monkey. It's playful and creative. Remember, there's no wrong way to write. Just write from your heart. Let's take some time to practise our rhymes. First, list down some things we could write a poem about!

Key Idea

POETRY: *A piece of writing to express your thoughts or feelings.*

We can write poems to express our thoughts or feelings. Many nursery rhymes are poems too! Poems can be simple. You do not have to use big words. Also, poems do not always have to rhyme. They can be about anything at all! The most important thing is to just express yourself!

There are a few points to keep in mind when you are planning to write your poem. Let's look at each of the points and the reasons why they are important to consider.

Title	What will your poem be about? What do you want to share with your reader?
Body	What are some important things you want to say? What are some thoughts or feelings you want to share in your poem?
Thoughts and feelings	How do you want your reader to feel after reading your poem?

Rhyme Time

Look at the list of words below. For each of the words given, write two to three words that rhyme in the space provided. Some hints have been given in the first column.

Word	Hint	A rhyming word	A rhyming word
Cat	_AT		
Sun	_UN		
Tree	_REE		
Ball	_ALL		
Fish	_ISH		
Cake	_AKE		
Book	_OOK		
Ring	_ING		
Car	_AR		
Hand	_AND		

Rhyme Time

Look at the list of words below. For each line, underline one or two words that rhyme with the given word.

Given word	Option 1	Option 2	Option 3
River	Giver	Pencil	Deliver
Forest	Best	Button	Rest
Mountain	Fountain	Elephant	Curtain
Whisper	Giraffe	Sister	Crisp
Thunder	Wonder	Sandwich	Under
Corner	Helmet	Blanket	Warmer
Ladder	Teacher	Bicycle	Climber
Ocean	Motion	Chocolate	Potion
Spider	Glider	Butterfly	Wider
Treasure	Pleasure	Lemonade	Measure

Answer Key

River	Giver	Pencil	Deliver
Forest	Best	Button	Rest
Mountain	Fountain	Elephant	Curtain
Whisper	Giraffe	Sister	Crisp
Thunder	Wonder	Sandwich	Under
Corner	Helmet	Blanket	Warmer
Ladder	Teacher	Bicycle	Climber
Ocean	Motion	Chocolate	Potion
Spider	Glider	Butterfly	Wider
Treasure	Pleasure	Lemonade	Measure

But... what if it doesn't rhyme perfectly? Will it still be a poem?
Rhyming is just one part of poetry. What matters most is the feeling and the fun in the words. Even if it doesn't rhyme perfectly, it's still poetry.
So, I can just play with words and see what happens? That sounds like fun! Let's make more rhymes!
Exactly! Think of all the things you love and start rhyming. You'll be surprised at how many words fit together.
And if you get stuck, don't worry. Just take a break and think about the sounds you want to hear. The rhymes will come to you.
Play with words, let them fly. Up, up, up, high in the sky!
You're doing great, everyone! Poetry is about expressing yourself, so let your imagination run wild. There's no limit to what you can create.
Wonderful work, team! Now, before we hear the wondrous rhymes and poems that are swimming around in your minds, let's work on brainstorming the poems first. To... the Rhyming Playground!

Rhyming Playground

Brainstorming

Here's an idea for a poem. Answer the guiding questions and draw a picture of the story in the box provided.

There is a monkey who loves learning and discovering new things.
One day, he goes on an adventure in the jungle.

What is the monkey's adventure like?

Question	Answer
What did the monkey experience with his five senses?	
What was the adventure about?	
Did he discover anything new? What happened in the end?	

Draw a picture of the monkey's adventure below.

Rhyming Playground

Brainstorming

Here's an idea for a poem. Answer the guiding questions and draw a picture of the story in the box provided.

There is a an elephant who can remember everything he sees. One day, he sees something special, which makes him recall a lovely memory.

What is the elephant's experience like?

Question	Answer
What did the elephant see? How can you describe it using the elephant's five senses?	
What special memory did the elephant recall?	
How did the special memory make the elephant feel? What did the elephant do?	

Draw a picture of the elephant's special experience below.

That was fun! I loved drawing out each story! What's next, what's next?
That's wonderful, Monkey. I loved seeing all of your drawings!
So, can I start writing now?
Yes! It's time to start writing your own poem. Since we are just starting out on this...
WAIT! What if I get stuck and don't know what to write?
This is why we're going back to the Rhyming Playground. If you get stuck, don't worry. Just take a break. Look at your drawings. Think about what words describe each picture. I'm sure the rhymes will come to you in no time at all!
Play with words, let them fly. Rhyme them here, rhyme them high!

Rhyming Playground

Comic sketch

Did you prefer the monkey's or the elephant's story on Pages 54 and 55? Draw the story you prefer as a comic strip in the boxes below.

1

2

3

4

5

6

Rhyming Playground

Pictures to words

Refer to your comic strip. For each picture, write a sentence that describes what is happening in the correct sequence of the story. You may choose to make the last word of the sentences rhyme. Turn to the next page for some helping words.

1

2

3

4

5

6

Rhyming Playground

Helping words

Sing	Ring
Happy	Friendly
Bright	Light
Cheer	Near
Voice	Choice
Learn	Turn
Adventure	Nature
Find	Kind
Explore	More
Discover	Cover
Remember	Tender
Memory	Story
See	Tree
Playful	Helpful
Spark	Park

Whoo-hoo!
I've arranged the words for you!

I did it! I did it! I did get a little stuck writing my poem about my adventure... But I referred to the helping words list and I did it!
That truly is fantastic, Monkey! There's just one more step to go.
I remembered this time! It's putting it all together!
Glad you're finally catching on! With all the building blocks of the activities we have done... Now you need to combine your rhymes and lines to nicely present your full poem!

Why are you helping them so much, Weasel? We're supposed to be messing things up for them!

My Wonderful Poem

Write your very own poem here.

Title of your poem	Write down your rhymes (if you want the poem to rhyme)

In a jungle full of green, the flowers shine so bright.
Parrot sings sweet songs from morning till night.
With rhythm and rhyme, she brings joy to me.
The animals gather, dancing around each tree.

Monkey swings high, he loves to play.
He claps his hands and starts to sway.
"I say, I say, I say,
good rhymes really make my day!"

CHAPTER 5

Building Blocks of Writing: Words and Vocabulary

It's important to choose words that you understand. Sometimes, simple words are the best choice. The key is to mix it up and find the right balance.
So, I can use different words to make my sentences more exciting, but I shouldn't make it too tricky? That sounds fun! I want to learn more new words!
That's right! I remember Coach saying that... Knowing more words gives you more tools to use in writing. Also, words can help you express your thoughts and feelings.
And if you learn a new word, try using it in a sentence right away. That's the best way to remember it and save it in your vocabulary bank.
New words, old words, mix them with care. Build your story everywhere!
Even if you sometimes forget a word, you can always look it up again.
I'm ready to build my vocabulary bank with lots of new words! This is going to be fun! Let's find some exciting words to use!
Great idea! Let's start with a puzzle... Try and see how many words you can spot!
I guess a thesaurus is not a dinosaur, Skunk?
Sorry about that! But... imagine meeting my great great great grandparents — the Skunkasaurus?
Get me out of here!

Word Quest

Monkey, Elephant and Parrot are exploring a jungle. They have experienced many different sights and sounds. In the word search below, look for the things they have discovered!

Monkey	Jungle	River	Rain	Trees
Parrot	Snake	Elephant	Leaves	Sunlight
Waterfall	Vines	Flowers	Explorer	Branch
Grass	Forest	Tiger	Bugs	Path

B	K	V	D	W	F	T	J	B	Q	U	A	F	J	R
C	G	R	G	J	R	L	S	H	X	P	Q	E	L	I
W	J	A	R	P	R	A	O	Y	T	A	E	B	E	V
A	U	I	A	P	A	X	R	W	R	T	I	E	A	E
T	N	N	S	B	E	R	B	U	E	H	S	X	V	R
E	G	B	S	U	L	V	R	B	E	R	X	P	E	K
R	L	R	F	G	E	I	F	O	S	P	S	L	S	T
F	E	A	O	S	P	N	X	S	T	I	U	O	E	N
A	N	N	R	P	H	E	K	U	M	N	M	R	H	R
L	Z	C	E	T	A	S	T	N	X	O	T	E	T	N
L	H	H	S	S	N	T	I	L	N	L	N	R	T	Y
I	D	J	T	N	T	X	G	I	Z	R	G	K	D	X
R	B	H	L	A	F	Z	E	G	L	F	A	R	E	I
U	A	Z	G	K	X	R	R	H	X	N	L	U	O	Y
N	K	V	W	E	A	U	L	T	S	T	J	P	P	E

Answer Key

B	K	V	D	W	F	T	J	B	Q	U	A	F	J	R
C	G	R	G	J	R	L	S	H	X	P	Q	E	L	I
W	J	A	R	P	R	A	O	Y	T	A	E	B	E	V
A	U	I	A	P	A	X	R	W	R	T	I	E	A	E
T	N	N	S	B	E	R	B	U	E	H	S	X	V	R
E	G	B	S	U	L	V	R	B	E	R	X	P	E	K
R	L	R	F	G	E	I	F	O	S	P	S	L	S	T
F	E	A	O	S	P	N	X	S	T	I	U	O	E	N
A	N	N	R	P	H	E	K	U	M	N	M	R	H	R
L	Z	C	E	T	A	S	T	N	X	O	T	E	T	N
L	H	H	S	S	N	T	I	L	N	L	N	R	T	Y
I	D	J	T	N	T	X	G	I	Z	R	G	K	D	X
R	B	H	L	A	F	Z	E	G	L	F	A	R	E	I
U	A	Z	G	K	X	R	R	H	X	N	L	U	O	Y
N	K	V	W	E	A	U	L	T	S	T	J	P	P	E

Words that rhyme, words that play, let them dance on the page today!
Wonderful poem, Parrot! And, great work, friends! It was so wonderful seeing how you worked together to find all the words.
Yes! That was fun!
Now, we're going to try something a little different — a crossword puzzle. It's another fun way to work with words.
What's a crossword puzzle? Is it like a word search?
It's easy! Solve the clues and write the correct word down in the boxes.
I'm ready to chirp out some answers! I love words!
I guess we'll need to think very carefully about each clue... to figure out the right word!
What if I get stuck and don't know the answer?
That's okay, Monkey. Just try your best! Remember, each clue gives a hint to help you. If you still need help, I'll be right here.
Alright, let's get started! I'm excited to try!
Skunk, I think you're the best crossword player I've ever met.
What do you mean? My worksheets have the most crosses in class! They're all wrong!
Exactly! Cross word — get it?
Why you little....

Key Idea

Why are words important?
Words help us talk, think and share ideas. They help us say what we feel, share what we see and talk to people about what we want to do. The more words you know, the better you can explain yourself and understand others!

What is vocabulary?
If someone has a wide vocabulary, they know lots of words! This is useful for speaking, reading and writing. Knowing many words makes it easier to talk about new things, tell stories and solve problems.

There are a few points to keep in mind when you are planning to write. Let's look at each of the points and the reasons why they are important to consider.

You can think about **G.R.O.W.** to remember how to use your words.

Every time you learn a new word, you become a better speaker, thinker and writer. Keep practicing and adding to your vocabulary. Keep growing!

G.R.O.W.

Gather	Collect new words from the books you read, people you talk to and words you hear around you.
Review	Write down the words and say them out loud. Find out what they mean too.
Organise	Sort your new words into groups, like feelings or actions. This will help you choose amazing words when you need to write!
Write	Practise using new words in your writing. This will help you understand and remember these new words!

Word Quest

Monkey, Elephant and Parrot are exploring a jungle. During the adventure, they found a puzzle. Can you help them identify the different words based on the clues below?

Across		Down	
1. Run fast	**4.** Low and deep animal sound	**2.** Loud and angry animal sound	**3.** Sound of something hitting the water
5. Lots of green plants	**6.** Jump far	**8.** Move through the air	**9.** Sneak around
7. Run after something	**10.** Untamed or free		

Answer Key

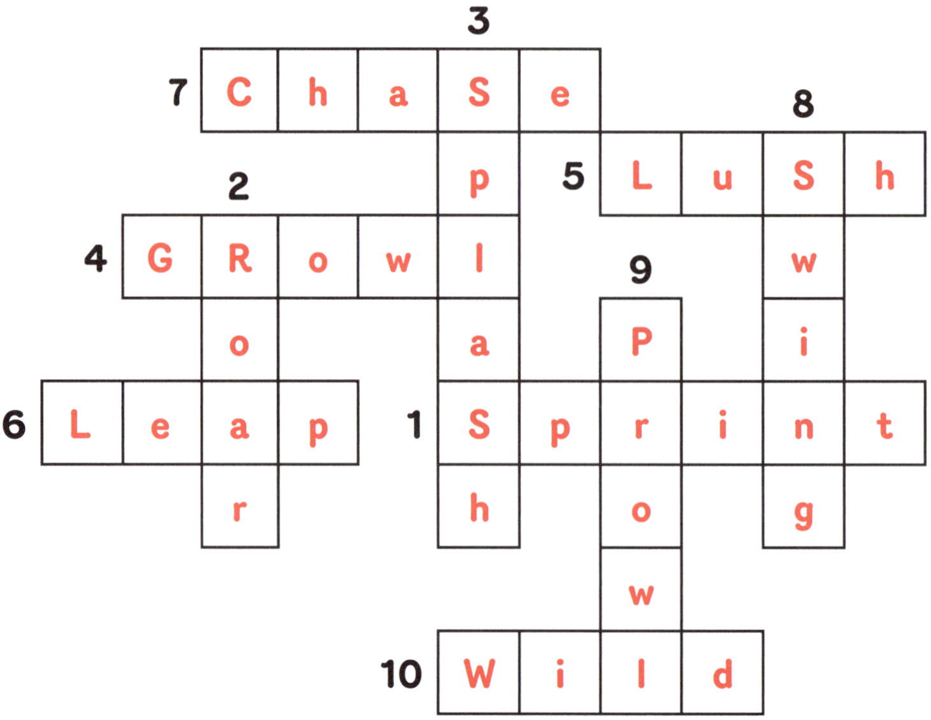
7 Chase
5 Lush
4 Growl
6 Leap
1 Sprint
10 Wild
3 Splash
2 Roar
8 Swing
9 Prowl

Well done, everyone! I knew you could do it! You all worked really hard figuring out those clues.
That was fun! But some of the clues were tricky...
You've gotten even better at solving them! Sometimes, we learn the most from the tricky ones.
I liked how the words fit tight, like a puzzle, just right. Clues and letters in a row, making pictures as we go!
Wonderful, Parrot! Speaking of connections, we're going to try something new.
What's next? More puzzles?
Not exactly... but we will still be working with words! Now, we're going to match words with their real meanings. This will help you understand new words even better. I'll give you a list of words on one side. I'll give some meanings on the other. Your job is to draw lines to match the word with its meaning.
So, we'll need to think about what each word means to find the right match. Just like when we solved the clues earlier!
What if I'm not sure about some of the meanings?
That's right! Think carefully. You might recognise some words from the crossword, but there will be new ones too. Take your time and get it right! Remember, there's no rush.

If you're unsure, look at all the choices. Look through all the meanings. It is all about learning and having fun with words.
I can't wait to shout and sing the right answers I will bring! Figuring out words is fun. Let's get started, everyone!
We love your enthusiasm, Parrot! Everyone ready? Let's get matching!

Word Quest

Monkey, Elephant and Parrot are writing a book on their jungle adventures! They have learnt many new words. Help them to use the words correctly by matching the correct meanings to each word.

Habitat •	• Blend in with surroundings
Pounce •	• Jump quickly on something
Jungle •	• Where an animal lives
Canopy •	• A thick forest
Predator •	• The top part of trees
Camouflage •	• Thick, full of plants
Dense •	• Run fast
Tropical •	• Jump far
Leap •	• A warm, rainy place
Sprint •	• An animal that hunts

Answer Key

Habitat	Blend in with surroundings
Pounce	Jump quickly on something
Jungle	Where an animal lives
Canopy	A thick forest
Predator	The top part of trees
Camouflage	Thick, full of plants
Dense	Run fast
Tropical	Jump far
Leap	A warm, rainy place
Sprint	An animal that hunts

Words are like treasures, shiny and bright.
They help us share stories with great delight.
With each new word, our stories grow.
Let's learn new words to make our stories go!

A verb or an adjective, they all have their place
in the sentences we write, they help us find space.
So let's play with words, explore and have fun.
Our pencils in our hands, we'll shine like the sun!

CHAPTER 6

Make Your Mark!

Commas, periods, stops, my dear! Use them and make your writing clear!
It's all about balance. Using too many exclamation marks can be too much. Just the right amount can add excitement to your story.
So, I can use different punctuation marks to make my story more exciting and easy to read? That sounds great! I want to try using them all!
That's right! Punctuation helps to tell your reader how to read your story the way you want it to be read.
And if you're ever unsure where to put a punctuation mark, just read your sentence out loud. Where you naturally pause or stop is usually where a mark should go!
Punctuation, oh what a treat, it makes your writing clear and neat!
Remember, it's okay to make mistakes while you're learning. The more you practise, the better you'll get at choosing the right punctuation marks. Who's ready to dive right in?
You heard that, Weasel? They're having a race.
What race? They're talking about punctuation marks!
On your marks, get set, go! Last one back is a rotten skunk!
Stop! Period! Comma! Pause this race!

Key Idea

PUNCTUATION: Punctuation marks are traffic lights in writing.

What is punctuation?
Punctuation marks are little marks that we need to include in writing. Examples of punctuations marks are periods/full stops (.), commas (,), question marks (?) and exclamation marks (!). These little marks may seem small, but they make a big difference in how someone else reads your writing.

Why is punctuation important?
Punctuation marks are like traffic lights in your writing. They help the reader know when to stop, when to pause and how to understand your sentences. Punctuation makes your writing clearer and easier to read!

Use T.A.P.S. to help you with punctuation marks in your writing.

T.A.P.S.

Talking markers	Use quotation marks ("___") to show when someone is talking.
Apostrophes	Use apostrophes (___'s) to show that something belongs to someone, e.g., Monkey's book. Apostrophes can also be used when you are leaving out letters, e.g., the words 'is not' can be shortened to isn't.
Pauses (commas)	Use commas (,) to show when there is a slight pause in your sentence.
Stop signs	Use periods (.), question marks (?) and exclamation marks (!) to end your sentence. These punctuation marks show where the sentence stops.

Punctuation Party

Elephant went on an adventure and wrote a short paragraph about it. As he was making a copy of the paragraph, he forgot to include the punctuation marks! Compare the two paragraphs to see the role of punctuation marks in writing.

Paragraph 1:

Elephant went on a big adventure in the jungle. He walked past tall green trees. He also splashed through a small river. Birds chirped in the sky above him. As he walked deeper into the jungle, Elephant found a secret waterfall. It was surrounded by bright flowers and long vines. He took a big gulp of water and felt refreshed. Suddenly, he heard rustling in the bushes. Elephant was curious, so he stepped closer. He found a family of monkeys playing nearby! They waved at him. Elephant smiled because he had made some new friends. It was a wonderful day full of surprises!

Paragraph 2:

Elephant went on a big adventure in the jungle he walked past tall green trees he also splashed through a small river birds chirped in the sky above him as he walked deeper into the jungle elephant found a secret waterfall it was surrounded by bright flowers and long vines he took a big gulp of water and felt refreshed suddenly he heard rustling in the bushes elephant was curious, so he stepped closer he found a family of monkeys playing nearby they waved at him elephant smiled because he had made some new friends it was a wonderful day full of surprises

Answer Key

Paragraph 2:
Elephant went on a big adventure in the jungle**(.)** ~~he~~ **He** walked past tall green trees**(.)** ~~he~~ **He** also splashed through a small river**(.)** ~~birds~~ **Birds** chirped in the sky above him**(.)** ~~as~~ **As** he walked deeper into the jungle**(,)** ~~elephant~~ **Elephant** found a secret waterfall**(.)** ~~it~~ **It** was surrounded by bright flowers and long vines**(.)** ~~he~~ **He** took a big gulp of water and felt refreshed**(.)** ~~suddenly~~ **Suddenly(,)** he heard rustling in the bushes**(.)** ~~elephant~~ **Elephant** was curious, so he stepped closer**(.)** ~~he~~ **He** found a family of monkeys playing nearby**(.)** ~~they~~ **They** waved at him**(.)** ~~elephant~~ **Elephant** smiled because he had made some new friends**(.)** ~~it~~ **It** was a wonderful day full of surprises**(!)**

Great job! Those two paragraphs should have given you a better understanding of punctuation. Did you notice how much easier it was to read the one with proper punctuation?
Yes! The first one made sense, but the second one was all mixed up! It was so hard to understand it without punctuation. Where did one idea end? When did another idea begin? It was so confusing!
Just remember... punctuation is like traffic signs. It helps us know when to stop or take a pause. When to slow down and when to speed up! Without it, things get confusing!
Exactly! Now that you've understood the difference, we're going to try something new. This time, I'll give you two more paragraphs. One will have proper punctuation, and the other will have mistakes.
We get to find the mistakes?
Yes! Your job will be to spot the errors and fix them. This will help you understand all of this even better.
I'm ready to sing out the right answers again!
Always so enthusiastic, Parrot! Let's see who can find and correct the punctuation mistakes first!

Punctuation Party

Monkey wrote a short paragraph about his adventure. As he was making a copy of the paragraph to share it with Elephant, he made mistakes with his punctuation marks! Compare the two paragraphs. Then, circle the punctuation marks that have been wrongly used.

Paragraph 1:

Monkey was excited to explore the jungle. He swung happily from branch to branch. He liked feeling the warm sun on his fur. As he jumped down from a tree, he spotted a colourful butterfly. Monkey was curious, so he decided to follow it. The butterfly led him to a hidden place filled with sweet fruits. Monkey tasted a juicy mango and squealed with delight. He picked a few fruits to share with his friends. Suddenly, he heard a rustle in the leaves. He turned to see Elephant walking towards him! They waved at each other. They were happy to enjoy the fruits together.

Paragraph 2:

Monkey was excited to explore the jungle. He, swung happily from branch to branch. He liked feeling the warm sun. on his fur. As he jumped down from a tree, he spotted a colourful butterfly. Monkey was curious, so he decided to follow it, The butterfly led him to a hidden place filled with sweet fruits" Monkey tasted a juicy mango and squealed with delight. He picked a few fruits to share with his friends. Suddenly. he heard a rustle in the leaves. He turned to see Elephant walking towards him! They, waved at each other. They were happy to, enjoy the fruits together.

Answer Key

Paragraph 2:

Monkey was excited to explore the jungle. He ~~(,)~~ swung happily from branch to branch. He liked feeling the warm sun ~~(.)~~ on his fur. As he jumped down from a tree, he spotted a colourful butterfly. Monkey was curious, so he decided to follow it~~(,)~~ **(.)** The butterfly led him to a hidden place filled with sweet fruits ~~(”)~~**(.)** Monkey tasted a juicy mango and squealed with delight. He picked a few fruits to share with his friends. Suddenly ~~(.)~~**(,)** he heard a rustle in the leaves. He turned to see Elephant walking towards him! They ~~(,)~~ waved at each other. They were happy to ~~(,)~~ enjoy the fruits together.

Well done! That was fantastic! You've just compared two paragraphs. One had correct punctuation, while the other one had mistakes.
Did you see how the one with correct punctuation was smoother and easier to read?
Yeah! The right punctuation made it easy to follow, but the other one felt like a bumpy ride full of unpleasant twists and turns.
Yes, it's like the wrong punctuation made the story hard to understand.
That's it! Punctuation helps our words flow and make sense. Now, you've practised spotting mistakes. For our last challenge, you'll get a paragraph with no punctuation at all!
No punctuation? That'll be tricky!
That's the fun part! Your job is to fill in the correct punctuation mark at the correct places. You already know the signs. Remember the T.A.P.S. So, let's see how well you can use them!
It's like putting together a puzzle, right?
That's right! You'll be the punctuation experts. Let's get started!

Punctuation Party

After Parrot saw Elephant's and Monkey's adventures, she decided to go on her own adventure! Unfortunately, she got so distracted with singing that she forgot about the punctuation marks!

Read Parrot's story:

Parrot flew high in the blue sky she looked for bright flowers to sing with Then she went down to a green jungle she saw friendly monkeys swinging from the trees the monkeys asked her to join their fun they danced and sang happy songs under the warm sun the monkeys liked Parrot's cheerful songs Soon they all gathered to listen Parrot flapped her wings and sang about the pretty flowers and tall trees the jungle was full of laughter and music everyone felt happy and free

Rewrite it in the lines given. While you rewrite it, add in the correct punctuation marks!

Answer Key

Read Parrot's story:

Parrot flew high in the blue sky**(.)** She looked for bright flowers to sing with**(.)** Then**(,)** she went down to a green jungle**(.)** She saw friendly monkeys swinging from the trees**(.)** The monkeys asked her to join their fun**(.)** They danced and sang happy songs under the warm sun**(.)** The monkeys liked Parrot's cheerful songs**(.)** Soon**(,)** they all gathered to listen**(.)** Parrot flapped her wings and sang about the pretty flowers and tall trees**(.)** The jungle was full of laughter and music**(!)** Everyone felt happy and free**(.)**

Periods stop sentences, nicely and neatly.
They tell us it's done, rather promptly.
Commas give pauses, a breath in between.
They help our writing flow, so smooth and clean.

Question marks ask things, with a little swirl,
"What's your favourite colour, ebony or pearl?"
Exclamation marks show excitement and cheer,
"Wow! What a great time! I'm so glad you're here!"

CHAPTER 7

Capitals of the World

Using a capital in the wrong place can make the word look odd or confusing. With practice, I'm sure you'll know just when to use them.
So, I can use capital letters to show the start of my sentences, names and special words? That sounds important! I want to try it out!
Exactly! Don't forget, every time you start a new sentence, it's like opening a new chapter with a capital letter.
If you're writing about yourself, the word 'I' is always capitalised. It's like giving yourself a little spotlight!
I, me, you and we, capital letters for you and me!
With practice, you'll know the rules so well. You'll be a capital letter expert in no time!
I'm ready to start using capital letters! My sentences are going to look so important and neat!
If you ever forget when to use a capital, just think about the start of a sentence or something important. Those are your clues!
Capitals here, capitals there, use them right, and show you care!
Fantastic work, team! Who's ready? First, we need to understand capital letters really well. On the next page, identify and circle the words that should start with a capital letter!
Ever wondered why capital letters never skip the queue?
Because they are nice letters?
Nope, because they always come first!
Oh, oh, oh, which letter appears in every name?
A capital letter!

Key Idea

CAPITAL LETTERS: Using capital letters in writing.

What are capital letters?

Using capital letters means using a big letter at the start of a word. We use capital letters at the beginning of sentences, for names, places and important things like the "Mr." in "Mr. Tan".

Why are capital letters important?

Capital letters are like signals in your writing that tell the reader to pay attention to certain words. Capital letters tell us when we're talking about important things, countries or people. They make your writing neat and clear!

Here are some examples of when you have to use capital letters.

Names	Always use capital letters for the names of people, countries and important things.
At the start of every sentence	Start every sentence with a capital letter.
Months and days	Remember to use capital letters for the days of the week and months of the year! For example, Monday or January.
Titles	When you write the title of a book or movie, you can start with a capital letter.

Capital Craze

Monkey and Elephant were reading a book on the different countries and cities of the world. However, Skunk and Weasel changed all the capital letters to small letters to confuse them. Help them as they figure this out! Circle all the words that should start with a capital letter.

singapore	run	sentosa	explore	zoo
tokyo	city	garden	bus	changi
lion	river	malaysia	beach	airport
orchard road	climb	merlion	eat	paris
amazon rainforest	windy	sing	thailand	beijing
school	sydney	jump	africa	discover

Answer Key

Singapore	run	**Sentosa**	explore	zoo
Tokyo	city	garden	bus	**Changi**
lion	river	**Malaysia**	beach	airport
Orchard Road	climb	**Merlion**	eat	**Paris**
Amazon Rainforest	windy	sing	**Thailand**	**Beijing**
school	**Sydney**	jump	**Africa**	discover

Fantastic job, everyone! I can see that you're becoming capital letter experts! Now, let's move on to something a little different...
Ooh, I'm excited! What's next, Coach?
Now you know when words need capital letters. Do you remember what a proper noun is?
Hmm... is it a special name, like someone's name or a place?
That's right, Monkey! A proper noun is a name of a specific person, place or thing. Like 'Mr. Green' or 'Singapore'. This type of word always needs a capital letter at the start.
So, for our next task, I'm going to give you a list of words. Some of them are common nouns, like 'chair' or 'car'. Some are proper nouns. Your job is to find which ones are the proper nouns and should start with capital letters.
I can do that! Proper nouns, here I come!
The tricky part is remembering when a word is just something general, like 'school' ... And when it's something special, like 'ABC School'. Only the actual name gets the capital letter.
Oh, I get it. So 'school' on its own doesn't need a capital, but 'ABC School' does, because it's the name of a particular school.
Exactly! That's a great example. Now, let's see how many proper nouns you can find on this list. Take your time and look carefully!
I'll be ready with a song when you get them all!
Alright! I'm going to find all the proper nouns first! I'll race you all!
We'll see about that, Monkey! I've got my eyes ready too.
Remember that proper nouns are names, so focus on those. Let's begin!

Capital Craze

You are now in a race with Monkey and Elephant! They managed to find all the proper nouns in just ten seconds! Do you think you can be faster? Circle the proper nouns where the first letter should be capitalised. The first one, 'James', has been done for you. Can you do it faster than Monkey and Elephant? Your time starts now!

tree	james	school	asia	pencil
orchard road	singapore river	car	london	marina bay sands
dog	mount everest	doctor	australia	book
sentosa	bird paradise	bicycle	brazil	flower
computer	tokyo	river	changi airport	uncle sam
garden	merlion	food	paris	lego

Answer Key

tree	**James**	school	**Asia**	pencil
Orchard Road	**Singapore River**	car	**London**	**Marina Bay Sands**
dog	**Mount Everest**	doctor	**Australia**	book
Sentosa	**Bird Paradise**	bicycle	**Brazil**	flower
computer	**Tokyo**	river	**Changi Airport**	**Uncle Sam**
garden	**Merlion**	food	**Paris**	**Lego**

Wow, everyone! You've done a fantastic job finding all those proper nouns. You have all really learned when to use capital letters for names. Now, it's time to take it to the next level!
That was fun! What's next, Coach?
Well, since you've all become experts... We're going to make it even more interesting. This time, you will be given a full sentence, but there's a catch!
A catch? Oh, I love surprises! What is it?
The sentence won't have any capital letters at all! Your job is to look at each sentence. Then, find the words that need a capital letter and fix them.
Exactly! And don't forget... proper nouns like people's names, places, and days of the week all need capital letters.
Oh! So we have to spot the proper nouns and the first word of the sentence?
I can do that! I'll find all the ones that need fixing!
I know you will! So let's get started with this final activity. Look at the sentences carefully, then fix the capital letters. Show me how sharp your skills are!

Capital Craze

You are so close to the finish line! Look at the sentences below. Rewrite each sentence with the correct capital letters.

my friend lives in london.

____

we visited the eiffel tower in paris.

____

my uncle visited singapore yesterday.

____

tokyo is the capital of japan.

____

the nile river flows through egypt.

____

my family flew to africa last year.

____

india is a busy country.

____

they went to malaysia.

____

mrs lee teaches in thailand.

____

i found a bear in the amazon rainforest.

____

Suggested Answers

my friend lives in london.

My friend lives in London.

we visited the eiffel tower in paris.

We visited the Eiffel Tower in Paris.

my uncle visited singapore yesterday.

My uncle visited Singapore yesterday.

tokyo is the capital of japan.

Tokyo is the capital of Japan.

the nile river flows through egypt.

The Nile River flows through Egypt.

my family flew to africa last year.

My family flew to Africa last year.

india is a busy country.

India is a busy country.

they went to malaysia.

They went to Malaysia.

mrs lee teaches in thailand.

Mrs Lee teaches in Thailand.

i found a bear in the amazon rainforest.

I found a bear in the Amazon Rainforest.

Capitals are special, they start with a glow.
Like names of our friends, or the places we know.
"Sentosa" shines bright and "Spider-Man" has flair.
When we write with capitals, we show that we care.

At the start of a sentence, a capital is the key.
It makes our ideas as clear as can be.
So remember to use them so your writing will shine.
With capital letters, your words will align!

CHAPTER 8

All Together Now!

If you want to add more information, you can add more! 'The monkey eats a banana while sitting on a tree.' Now it's a bit more detailed.
Whether they're short or long, keep your sentences clear and strong!
I get it! A sentence needs all its parts to make sense. So, if I just say 'banana,' it's not really a sentence! It doesn't tell the whole story.
That's right, Monkey. 'Banana' is just a word, but 'The monkey eats a banana.' is a complete sentence. It tells us what's happening.
Sentences are the building blocks of our whole story.
Start with a thought, make it clear, every sentence should have a complete idea!
Exactly, Parrot! Sentences give your words meaning and help your readers understand your ideas.
I want to try! Can I? I'll start with 'The monkey eats a banana.', and then I can add more to make it a longer sentence!
That's the spirit! Start simple. Then, add more details as you go. It's like building with blocks — one piece at a time to build a tall and strong tower!
And, if you ever get stuck, just remember the basics: subject, verb (action) and object. That's all you need to make a strong sentence.
Put it all together, words in line, make a sentence every time!

Wonderful work, team! Remember, each sentence is a step towards telling your story. Let's see what you can create!
I'm ready to start! My sentences are going to tell a whole story by the time I'm done!
Every sentence is a chance to share your ideas clearly. Let's put those words to work!
Hey, Weasel, look at what they're doing. They're working on sentences.
Let's mix them up!
Words the up mix?
Exactly! Mix up the words. I think they have a worksheet in the next few pages. Let's get to it before they do!
You jumble them up! I'll steal the full stops!

Key Idea

ORGANISING OUR SENTENCES: Writing sentences in different ways.

What is a sentence?
A sentence is a group of words that shares a complete idea. Every sentence needs a subject (this refers to who or what the sentence is about) and a verb (this often refers to what the subject is doing). For example, 'Parrot sings.' Parrot is the subject and sings is the verb.

Why is it important to organise our sentences well?
When your sentences are clear, your writing is easier to understand. It helps readers to follow your story or idea easily.

Use S.A.V.E.D. to help you build clear sentences!

S.A.V.E.D.

Start clearly	What do you want your sentence to be about? This should be very clear to you. For example, a sentence could start with a subject like "Elephant", "Monkey" or "Parrot."
Actions and **V**erbs	What is the action in the sentence? Use a verb to show what is happening in the sentence. What is your subject doing? For example, "Elephant is studying."
End with a period or full stop	Always end your sentence with a period or full stop (.), question mark (?) or exclamation mark (!).
Details	You can add more details to make your sentences interesting. You can use words to show how the action is being done. For example, "Parrot sings ***loudly***." Another way is to add more details about the place or other people around. For example, "Parrot sings on the top of the mountain." or "Parrot sings for Monkey and Elephant."

All Jumbled Up

Monkey and Elephant are trying to read a book. Unfortunately, Skunk and Weasel jumbled up the words. Can you help them out? Look at the words below. Rearrange and rewrite them in the correct order and don't forget the full stops!

Parrot tree on sat the

____

bananas ate the yellow Monkey

____

Elephant water drank river from the

____

flew Parrot high sky the in

____

saw Monkey a coconut tree tall

____

and Parrot colourful has feathers bright

____

footprints Elephant behind the left big

____

jungle the together explored friends The

____

Did you remember your capital letters and full stops?

Answer Key

Parrot tree on sat the

Parrot sat on the tree.

bananas ate the yellow Monkey

Monkey ate the yellow bananas.

Elephant water drank river from the

Elephant drank water from the river.

flew Parrot high sky the in

Parrot flew high in the sky.

saw Monkey a coconut tree tall

Monkey saw a tall coconut tree.

and Parrot colourful has feathers bright

Parrot has colourful and bright feathers. / Parrot has bright and colourful feathers.

footprints Elephant behind the left big

Elephant left behind the big footprints.

jungle the together explored friends The

The friends explored the jungle together.

Great job moving those words around! Now you all know how to build a simple sentence. But… what if we want to make our sentences more exciting?
Ooh, can we add more words to say where things happen?
Or when things happen! I like that! Maybe even why something is happening!
Bingo! In this next activity, we're going to take simple sentences and make them interesting by adding more details. You can add where, when, how or even why something happens. Your sentences can become more interesting with these details!
We'll need to use our memory for this. I'm trying hard now to think of words I can add to make my sentences super exciting! I know that words can paint a picture in our minds.
I'm ready! Let's make our sentences fun and wonderful!
Add in a word or maybe three, to make it fun as it can be! A sentence long, with sounds so sweet, will make this task a joyful feat!
That's the spirit! Don't be afraid to get creative. Let's see who can make the most interesting sentence. Use your imagination and add in those details! Who's ready for the challenge?
Me, me! I can do it! I'll make my sentences the most wonderful sentences in the whole wide world!
Alright, let's get started. Show me how much you can stretch those sentences!

Bigger and Better

Monkey and Elephant are trying to make some sentences more interesting! Unfortunately, they are out of ideas. Can you help them? Look at the sentences below. Rewrite each sentence and add on more details. Two examples have been done for you.

Monkey climbed a tree.
Example: Monkey climbed a tall tree to look for bananas.

Elephant splashed water.
Example: Elephant splashed water at Monkey on a hot afternoon.

Parrot sang a song. *(Who did Parrot sing for?)*

____

Monkey found a banana. *(Where did Monkey find it?)*

____

Parrot flew over the jungle. *(When did Parrot fly over the jungle?)*

____

Elephant trumpeted loudly. *(Why did Elephant trumpet loudly?)*

____

Monkey threw a stone. *(Where did Monkey throw the stone?)*

____

Elephant discovered a lake. *(When did Elephant discover the lake?)*

____

Monkey swung on a vine. *(Why did Monkey swing on a vine?)*

____

Monkey made a funny face. *(Who did Monkey make a funny face at?)*

____

Suggested Answers

Parrot sang a song. *(Who did Parrot sing for?)*

Parrot sang a song for Monkey.

Monkey found a banana. *(Where did Monkey find it?)*

Monkey found a banana hanging on the tree branch.

Parrot flew over the jungle. *(When did Parrot fly over the jungle?)*

Parrot flew over the jungle in the evening.

Elephant trumpeted loudly. *(Why did Elephant trumpet loudly?)*

Elephant trumpeted loudly because he saw a mouse.

Monkey threw a stone. *(Where did Monkey throw the stone?)*

Monkey threw a stone into the river.

Elephant discovered a lake. *(When did Elephant discover the lake?)*

Elephant discovered a lake last week.

Monkey swung on a vine. *(Why did Monkey swing on a vine?)*

Monkey swung on a vine as he searched for bananas.

Monkey made a funny face. *(Who did Monkey make a funny face at?)*

Monkey made a funny face at Parrot.

Wow, those sentences are fantastic! You all did an amazing job adding details. You really made them more exciting!
I think we've really stretched our sentences to their limits. What's next, Coach?
Now that you're all sentence experts, let's take things up a level! In this next activity, we're going to combine two sentences into one.
Combine? You mean like putting two sentences together?
Exactly! Sometimes, instead of having two short sentences, you can join them to make one longer, smoother sentence.
Two ideas that become just one. It's like combining words for fun! We join them up with care, you see, and make them flow so naturally!
We'll need to think carefully about how to connect the ideas. Should we use a word like 'and' or 'because'?
Yes, exactly. Words like 'and', 'but' or 'because' help to connect the ideas. Let's see how well you can combine two short sentences into one. Ready to try this out?
Ready! I'm going to make these sentences even better!
Wonderful! Let's jump right in and see who can come up with the best and most wonderful sentences!

Better Together

Monkey and Elephant are trying to combine some sentences! Unfortunately, they are out of ideas again. Can you help them? Look at the sentences below. Combine the two sentences using the word in the bracket. Two examples have been done for you.

Monkey found a shiny rock.
Monkey showed it to Elephant. (**and**)

*Example: Monkey found a shiny rock **and** showed it to Elephant.*

Elephant bathed in the lake.
It was a hot afternoon. (**because**)

*Example: Elephant bathed in the lake **because** it was a hot afternoon.*

Monkey swung from tree to tree.
Monkey was looking for his friends. (**because**)

____

Elephant stomped through the jungle.
Elephant knocked over some trees. (**and**)

____

Monkey and Elephant danced together.
They were very happy. (**because**)

____

Monkey picked some bananas from a tree.
Monkey wanted to share the bananas with his friends. (**because**)

____

Parrot sang happily.
Parrot danced happily. (**and**)

____

Suggested Answers

Monkey swung from tree to tree.
Monkey was looking for his friends. (**because**)

Monkey swung from tree to tree because he was looking for his friends.

Elephant stomped through the jungle.
Elephant knocked over some trees. (**and**)

Elephant stomped through the jungle and knocked over some trees.

Monkey and Elephant danced together.
They were very happy. (**because**)

Monkey and Elephant danced together because they were very happy.

Monkey picked some bananas from a tree.
Monkey wanted to share the bananas with his friends. (**because**)

Monkey picked some bananas from a tree because he wanted to share the bananas with his friends.

Parrot sang happily.
Parrot danced happily. (**and**)

Parrot sang and danced happily.

A sentence is a party, with words that come to play.
They go hand in hand to dance happily every day.
Start with a subject, the star of the show.
Then add in the action, and watch the fun flow!

Use words in a pattern, like you're building a tower.
Each one is important, together they will flower.
Good sentences have a nice ring.
Oh, what lovely stories they bring!

CHAPTER 9

Talking About the Weather

Rain can pour, rain can fall. Use your words to say it all!
You can also talk about how the weather makes you feel!
I get it! So, if it's a bright, sunny day, I could say 'The warm sun made me feel happy and relaxed.' That describes both the weather and how it affects me!
Exactly! Descriptive words add depth to your writing, making it more interesting and engaging for your readers.
And remember, you can mix and match words to create unique descriptions. For example, 'the icy wind kissed my cheeks'.
Words to show, words to feel, make your weather reports real!
That's the spirit, Parrot! Use your descriptive words to paint any image you want. Let's get creative with our weather words!
I'm ready to try! I'm going to describe a stormy day and make it sound really dramatic!
I'll give you a list of weather conditions, like 'cloud'. I'll also give you some fun descriptive words, like 'colourful' or 'fluffy'. Your job is to match the right word to each noun.
Like matching 'fluffy' with 'cloud'?
Yes, just like that! Let's jump right in and match those words. Are you ready?

Key Idea

DESCRIBING THE WEATHER: Talking about the weather in your stories.

Why is the weather important?
How do you feel on a cool and windy day? What about a rainy day when there is thunder and lightning? The weather can help to create a special setting in your story. It can make your writing more exciting too. For example, if it suddenly starts to rain in your story, your characters might have a problem if they do not have any umbrellas!

How can you describe the weather?
Use different words to share what the weather is like. Is it sunny, rainy or windy? How does the weather make the characters feel? Does it make the characters happy, scared or tired? You can make your story more exciting by talking about how the weather feels, looks and sounds.

Remember **W.E.A.T.H.E.R.** to help you use describe the weather in your story

W.E.A.T.H.E.R.

Wind	Describe the wind. Is it strong? Could it be a light breeze? Perhaps it is a hot day without any wind at all?
Earth	Describe the earth or sand under your feet. Is it wet or dry? Is it hot or cold?
Air	Describe the air around you. Is it warm or cold?
Temperature	Describe the temperature. Is it a hot or cold day?
Humidity	Describe whether the weather makes you perspire a lot. Talk about whether the weather is humid or cool.
Emotions	Describe the emotions that the weather makes you feel.
Rain	Describe whether it is raining or sunny.

Painting the Weather

Monkey and Elephant are having an argument over the weather. Monkey thinks that it is correct to say "dark rain". On the other hand, Elephant insists that "fluffy sun" is correct. Can you help them out?
Look at the nouns and the descriptive words. Match two descriptive words for each noun to correctly describe them.

Bright	Strong	Bright	Dark	Heavy
Gentle	Howling	Violent	Fierce	Hot

Sky	

Rain	

Sun	

Wind	

Storm	

Suggested responses

Sky	
Bright	Dark

Rain	
Heavy	Gentle

Sun	
Bright	Hot

Wind	
Howling	Strong

Storm	
Violent	Fierce

Wow, that was great! I can see you're all getting better at describing the weather.
That was fun! What's next?
Next, we're going to take it up a level. I will need you to read some lines that Parrot has written. She has been having some trouble finding the right words to describe what she saw on her adventure.
Right or wrong, short or long, choose the best one, writing is so fun!
Wait, how do we make Parrot's sentences better?
Great question, Elephant! Imagine you have a tiny seed… a sentence like 'It was the afternoon.' Also, you know that it was so hot that no one wanted to play outside. Now, how can you make it bloom with more details?
Oh, I know! We can say how hot it is! Like, 'It was an unbearably hot afternoon, so people stayed inside.'
Exactly, Monkey! Add details like what the weather was or how it felt like… anything that paints a clearer picture in our minds.
So, we're adding colours to the sentence with words! Like painting a picture with details.
That's right! You're not just telling a story, you're creating a whole picture that we can imagine.
Paint with words, make it bright. Add more colour, make it right!
This sounds fun!
Yes! I've given you some helping words to use!
I can't wait to help Parrot grow her sentences with more colour!
Let's get started then! Pick a sentence, and let's see how colourful you can make it. Ready?

Colour the Weather

Parrot is flying high up above the trees. She enjoys looking around and watching what is going on around the jungle. As she tries to write down what she sees, she gets stuck! She needs some help to fill in the blanks with descriptive words to add more colour to her writing! The first letter has been provided as a clue for you.

sunny	gloomy	strong	cool
perfect	blazing	glorious	poor
heavy	chilly	breezy	weak

1. The sun was shining brightly on the **s**____________ day, making Monkey very happy.
2. It was a **p**____________ afternoon for Elephant to take a stroll on the beach.
3. Parrot loved the **c**____________ breeze as she flew high in the sky.
4. A **h**____________ rain started to fall, so Monkey ran for cover.
5. The sky turned **g**____________ as dark clouds gathered before the storm.
6. It felt **b**____________ outside. Everyone was sweating from the heat.
7. The **c**____________ air made Elephant feel a little cold.
8. The **b**____________ weather was perfect for Monkey to fly a kite.
9. Parrot sang a beautiful song after seeing a **g**____________ sunset.
10. A **s**____________ wind blew through the jungle. It made all the leaves shake.

Answer Key

1. The sun was shining brightly on the (sunny) day, making Monkey very happy.
2. It was a (perfect) afternoon for Elephant to take a stroll on the beach.
3. Parrot loved the (cool) breeze as it flew high in the sky.
4. A (heavy) rain started to fall, so Monkey ran for cover.
5. The sky turned (gloomy) as dark clouds gathered before the storm.
6. It felt (blazing) outside. Everyone was sweating from the heat.
7. The (chilly) air made Elephant feel a little cold.
8. The (breezy) weather was perfect for Monkey to fly a kite.
9. Parrot sang a beautiful song after seeing a (glorious) sunset.
10. A (strong) wind blew through the jungle. It made all the leaves shake.

Sunny days are bright, with a golden glow.
Raindrops softly fall and help the flowers grow.
The wind whispers sweetly, whooshing through the trees.
The snowflakes dance gently, like tiny white bees.

Clouds can be fluffy, like cotton candy in the sky.
Stormy skies rumble, as the loud thunder rolls by.
Descriptive words help us to share what we see.
Let's paint the weather with words full of glee!

CHAPTER 10

My Best Friend!

Characters who care, characters who dare. Build them with love, help them rise above!
I'm ready to create my character! I'm going to give them a big dream and a little secret that they don't want anyone to know.
That sounds great! You could also talk about something that they learn at the end of the story.
And, don't forget to share something your character has experienced in the past that makes them who they are!
Give them a past, give them a tale, make them strong or make them frail!
I can't wait to start! My character is going to be the most interesting person ever!
Not if I have anything to say about it! My character will be the best!
Hey, Weasel, who's your favourite character?
From games or books or movies?
Wow, from games?
You can see how game creators come up with very interesting characters in games too. I like Leon or Crow from Brawl Stars because they look cool. My favourite character in a book would be difficult because I have so many...
Do you like the good guys or the bad guys?
Oh, the bad guys make the story much more interesting. I don't like them all, but they're important for the story.
Do you think you're a bad guy? Because you're a Weasel and you steal food from Monkey and Elephant?
What? No! I mean, yes, but I was just trying to see how they taste.
Well... what are you waiting for? Let me see how they taste too!

Key Idea

CHARACTERS: Talking about the characters in your stories.

Why are characters important?
Characters are an important part of any story. Characters allow people to imagine themselves being in the story. If people are able to imagine themselves in the story, they will enjoy reading your story even more!

How to describe a character?
To describe a character well, you need to talk about a few different parts of the character. Physical appearance is one easy way to help readers imagine how your character looks like without looking at any picture! Other parts about a character that you should share with your readers are the character's personality, relationships with others and their past experiences.

Remember **C.A.R.E.** to help you describe the characters in your story.

C.A.R.E.

Character traits	Talk about what kind of person your character is. What is something about their personality that you can share? For example, is he/she kind, funny or brave?
Appearance	Talk about how your characters look. Are they tall? What is their hairstyle like? What clothes are they wearing? Does he/she have something unique, like a special scar?
Relationships	How is his/her relationship like with friends and family? Do they get along well? What do they like about each other?
Experiences	What happened to your character in the past? Was there a special experience he/she went through? Did he/she face a tough problem? What did he/she learn from it?

Character Craft

Monkey and Elephant are having a competition over who can create the most interesting character. Can you create a more interesting character than theirs?

Firstly, give your character a name. Look at the character traits list. Select two traits and write them in the boxes below. After that, write one sentence which describes something that this character would do. Refer to the example below.

Traits			
Brave	Kind	Funny	Curious
Helpful	Friendly	Honest	Adventurous

Name of your character	Trait	Sentence
Bob	Kind	Bob helped the old lady carry her heavy bags.

Great job, everyone! You've picked some amazing traits for your characters.
I can't wait to see how everyone's characters will look! I'm sure they'll be full of life!
What's next, Coach? How are we going to bring our characters to life?
Now it's time to draw your character. Think about what they look like. What fun things do they like to do?
Ooh, I love to sing! I'll make my character a singer with a shiny microphone!
That sounds fantastic, Parrot! Remember, your drawing can show us your character's traits.
After we draw them, what should we write about?
Great question, Elephant! After you draw, you'll write a few sentences to describe your character.
What does your character look like? What's their favourite activity? And how do they show their traits?
I can't wait to see what everyone will make! This activity will be a piece of cake!
Yes! Let's make our drawings and stories exciting.
Yes! I want to see all your creativity. Let's get started! Have fun creating your wonderful characters!

Character Craft

Answer these guiding questions, then draw the character you have created.

Question	Answer
What is his/her hair like? What colour is his/her hair? How long/short is it?	
What is he/she wearing? What colour or pattern or style?	
What special features does your character have?	
What facial expression does your character usually have? Is he/she happy, sad, angry or fierce?	

Wow, everyone! Your drawings and descriptions are amazing! I can really see your characters come to life.
I loved drawing mine! She's brave and always helps her friends!
I had a great time writing about my character's favourite things. He loves climbing trees!
I made my character a superstar! She loves to sing and dance, oh how bizarre!
Fantastic work, everyone! Next, we're going to be even more creative.
What are we doing, Coach?
Look at the traits and details from your drawings and descriptions. Use that to write a short story about your character!
That sounds fun! Can we make it an adventure?
Absolutely! What would your character do in a special situation?
I can't wait to write about my character's big concert!
Let's get started! I'm excited to see the adventures you'll create!

Story Time

Draw a picture of your character facing a problem.

What is happening to your character in the story?

Characters are special, each one is unique,
with funny quirks and wishes that they seek.
Monkey is brave, swinging high with a laugh.
Elephant is so gentle, with a heart full of love.

Parrot loves to sing, with feathers so bright.
They go on adventures both day and night.
Let's make them exciting, with traits that shine.
Our interesting characters, one story at a time!

CHAPTER 11

My Favourite Movies

At the heart of every great movie is a story that we care about.
So, what makes a movie story different from a book story? Is it just the pictures and sounds?
Movies can show us things in a way books can't, with moving images and sounds. The important thing is that the story itself still needs to be strong.
A good movie has an exciting story and interesting characters... just like a good book.
A story so true, a plot so grand. In a movie, it's all close at hand!
The setting helps set the mood and tone of the story, whether it's spooky, exciting or adventurous.
I want to write a story like a movie! One with lots of action and surprises!
You can do that, Monkey! Just remember to keep your characters and plot in mind as you write.
And think about how you can use words to create colourful pictures in your reader's mind, just like a movie does with its images.
Use your words to make it clear, a movie in their mind, so near!
That's the spirit, Parrot! Movies and stories both have the power to take us on incredible adventures. Now, let's see what kind of stories you can create!

Key Idea

PROBLEMS IN A STORY: Talking about the problems a character might face.

Why are problems important in stories?
Every story needs a problem for the character to solve. A problem makes the story more exciting. This is because a problem helps readers see how the character changes or learns something new. Problems can make the character's journey more interesting for the reader.

How to talk about the problems in a story?
The problem should be something important to the character. Maybe they have lost something, need to help someone or have to make a tough decision. The way the character handles the problem is what makes the story fun to read.

Remember **P.A.T.H.** to help you talk about problems in your story.

P.A.T.H.

Present the problem	What happens in the story that creates the problem? What is the problem? Does the character need to find something? Is it a challenge he/she needs to overcome?
Affect the character	How does the problem affect your characters? Does it stop them from getting something they want? How do the characters feel about the problem? Are they angry, sad, determined or nervous?
Try to solve it	What is the first thing your character does to fix the problem? For example, does he/she make a plan, get help or come up with a new idea?
How it ends	Does your character's plan work? What else can he/she try to fix the problem? How does he/she finally solve the problem? What does your character learn from this experience?

Character Craft

Think of your favourite movie character. Then, answer these guiding questions. Lastly, draw this character on the next page.

Your favourite movie or book or game:	Your character's name:
Question	**Answer**
What does the character look like? What colour is his/her hair? How long/short is it? What is the style like?	
What is he/she wearing? What colour or pattern or style?	
What special features does your character have? Does he/she have a special accessory or scar?	
What facial expression does your character usually have? Is he/she happy, sad, angry, fierce or gentle?	
What is one thing the character does that you like?	
What is something the character likes to say?	

Great job, everyone! I loved hearing about your amazing movie characters. They're unique and full of life! Now, let's think about what happens to these characters in a story.
How do we do that, Coach?
We're going to create a plot map! This will help us outline the beginning, middle and end of a movie featuring your character.
Sounds exciting! What should we write? Let's make it clear and keep it bright!
Do we think about the character's feelings, too?
Yes, Elephant! Share how the character feels when he or she faces the problem. You want your audience to feel connected to your character.
Can we use pictures for our plot map?
Absolutely! Feel free to draw different important things in the story. Let's get creative!
I can't wait to start mapping out my character's journey!
Alright, everyone! Grab your materials, and let's dive into your plot maps!

Problem-o-matic

Answer these questions to explore what problem the character faces in your story. Then, draw a scene of your character facing this problem!

Question	Answer
What is the problem?	
What does the character find difficult?	
How does the character feel about this problem?	
What does the character try to do to solve the problem?	

Fantastic work on your character's problem! I can already see how your characters will shine in their stories. Now, it's time to write!
What should we write about?
Good question, Monkey! You have already written about your characters and the problems they face.
Finally, now, we have the ending. Tell us about how the character solved the problem!
I like that idea! It's truly smart. It helps us show the story's heart!
Exactly! Remember, answer each question to go deeper into how the problem is solved.
What if I get stuck while writing?
No worries! You can always look back at your character in the previous activities for guidance. Plus, I'll be here to help if you need any support.
This is going to be fun! I'm excited to see how all the problems get solved!
Me too! Let's get our ideas flowing and start writing. Remember to let your imagination lead the way!

Saving the Day

Answer these questions to explore how the problem is resolved. Then, draw a scene of your character solving this problem!

Question	Answer
What is the first thing the character tries to do to solve the problem?	
Will this idea work immediately? (Remember that if it does, the story will end very quickly.)	
Who helps the character to try to solve the problem?	
What special skill or knowledge does the character have that helps him/her solve the problem? E.g., a special power to do something	
What does the character learn from solving the problem?	

Every story has a problem, whether big or small.
It could be a monkey who slips and starts to fall.
It could be an elephant who can't find its snack.
Or a parrot lost in the jungle, flying off track.

But don't you worry, because solutions are near.
With teamwork and courage, we won't have to fear.
Together we'll solve it, with smiles and cheer,
turning big problems into fun stories here!

CHAPTER 12

My Favourite Books

In forests deep or castles grand, settings take us by the hand!
I want to write a great story that everyone will remember! One with characters and adventures that people won't forget!
Me too! Me too!
You both can, my friends! Just remember to put your heart into it! Think about what makes your favourite stories so special.
Use your words with care and might, make your story shine so bright!
That's the spirit! Every great story has its own flavour. Now, let's see the unforgettable stories you create!
First, let's look at characters. You have done this before. So, I'm expecting something even more special this time!
Yes, Coach! I am going to create a brand new character just for this!
I remember that to create a character, we need to describe...
The character's traits, appearance...
Their relationship with others and something that they experienced in the past! C-A-R-E... CARE!

That's right, my clever friends. Follow what you've learnt in C.A.R.E. to create your wonderful, interesting characters!
Are you ready, Elephant? Let's see who can make the more interesting character!
Weasel… I'm not sure why, but I'm feeling a little sad.
What's wrong?
I don't know… it's like I know something is going to happen…
You're making me sad too, Skunk. We've been through 11 chapters together already. You can tell me anything…
That's alright. Maybe I just need some time alone.

Key Idea

SOLUTIONS IN A STORY: Talking about how problems are solved in your stories.

Why are solutions important in stories?
After your character faces a problem, the story needs a solution. A good solution can make your story very interesting! The solution shows how the character overcomes the challenge. Solutions also help you to end your story well. It can also show how the character grows or learns something new.

How to talk about solutions?
A good solution doesn't always come easily. Sometimes, you have to make your character work hard for the solution. The character might even need to fail before succeeding. It is often more exciting when the characters do not solve the problem on their first try! The solution should make sense based on what your character knows, feels or learns during the story.

Remember **P.L.A.N.** to help you talk about solutions in your story:

P.L.A.N.

Plan	How does your character try to solve the problem? What is the first thing he/she does? Does he/she try to come up with an idea or get help from someone?
Learn	What will your character learn after failing the first time? What will your character learn after solving the problem?
Achieve	What will your character achieve in the end?
Next step	What happens in the end after everything is done? How will the story end?

Character Craft

It's time to create your unique character! Answer the questions to help you explore what makes your character so special.

Question	Answer
What is your character's name?	
What is one special skill your character has?	
What is your character's favourite food?	
What is one secret your character has? (This secret can make him/her extra special.)	
What clothes does your character wear?	
What is his/her hairstyle like?	
Does your character have any special scar or accessory? What is it?	

Write a short paragraph telling everyone about your character. Use your answers to the questions!

Great job, everyone! Your characters are full of life and creativity. I loved how each one has a unique personality. Now, let's take a step further. We're going to think about where our characters live… their setting!
Yes! A good story needs a great place. We want to know what it looks like, smells like and even sounds like!
Can we make our settings as fun as our characters? I want to create a magical forest with sparkling rivers, colourful flowers and beautiful birds!
Oh, what a sight! With colours so bright, they light up the night. Yes, the magical birds take flight!
Absolutely! You can add whatever you like. For the next activity, you'll create your character's setting. Think about it… how does it make your character feel?
I'm excited! My character loves to explore. So, the setting will be important for their adventure. I think my character will feel so excited being in a cave!
Exactly! Use your imagination to create an exciting place for your character. Remember, the setting can be like a character itself. The setting helps to decide how your story unfolds.
Can we use colours and sounds to make our settings even more exciting?
Definitely! Imagine being there. Using your five senses, add as many details as you can. This will help your readers to imagine being there! Let's get started… I can't wait to see what you create!

Story World

Question	Answer
Where does your story happen? E.g., home, forest, school, field	
What are the most important things you see in the place? E.g., tables in the canteen or classroom	
What sounds can you hear? E.g., children laughing and playing	
What do you smell? E.g., food in the canteen	
What makes this place special? E.g., a place where I meet my friends	

Write a short paragraph telling everyone about your setting. Use your answers to the questions!

Great job, everyone! Your characters are really interesting. Now, let's think about what happens to them in the story.
You mean... What kind of problem they have?
Yes, Monkey! Every story has a problem the character has to fix. It could be something big, like getting lost...
Or something smaller, like losing a toy. The problem makes the story exciting!
The problem makes the story fun, the action fast, the story run. What will they do? How will it end? Let's see how things will bend!
Oh yes, I remember problems in all the stories. That's why I keep reading... I always want to see how it ends!
Exactly! Now, let's give your characters a challenge. In the next activity, you'll need to do two things. First, think of a problem. Then, think of how your character will solve it. Will it be easy or hard? Let's see what you come up with!
I'm ready! My character's going to have a big challenge!
That's the spirit, Monkey! Let's start by thinking about a problem, then a solution. Ready, everyone?

Problem-o-matic

Your character experiences some trouble! Answer the questions to help you explore what the problem is... and how your character solves it!

Question	Answer
How did this problem happen? (Did he/she lose something? Did he/she make a mistake?)	
Why is this problem important? (Does it stop your character from getting something? How does it make him/her feel?)	
What does your character do to solve the problem?	
Does the plan work? If not, what does he/she try next?	
How is the problem solved? What does your character learn from this?	

Write a short paragraph telling everyone about your character's problem. Use your answers to the questions!

Wow! You've all come up with some great problems and clever solutions for your characters. Now, it's time to put it all together!
So, what do we do next? Are we going to make the whole story?
Yes, Monkey! You've already created your characters, their settings and their problems. Now, we're going to work on the whole story. Who remembers...
I remember! We need a start, a middle and an end to make our story complete.

Yes, you've got it! You have already done the hard part! You have created your character. You've created a beautiful and exciting setting. In this next activity, look at everything you've done and combine them to write your story! This will help you see how the story flows from one part to the next.
First, the start, where it all begins. Then the middle, where the fun spins! At the end, what will they do? Solve the problem, say 'phew'!

That sounds fun! I can't wait to see my story come together.
Let's get ready, everyone. After writing your masterpiece, you will draw out your story! I can't wait to see your stories and drawings come to life!

Final Masterpiece

Your story is almost complete! Describe your characters, setting, problem and solution on the lines below. Then, draw what happens in your story in the boxes!

Draw what happens in your story in these boxes!

I think I know why I'm so sad, Weasel...
I know why, Skunk... I'm feeling it too. It's the last chapter!
Do you think we'll see these animals and friends again?
I don't know but I certainly hope so.
Bye bye, my jungle friends. Let this not be the end. Go write your stories, yes, you can! We will see you right around the bend!

When a problem appears, we don't despair.
Like Elephant who just lost his favourite chair,
with friends around him, they think and plan.
They'll find a way, together they can!

Monkey helps, climbing high with all his might,
Parrot shares ideas that are wonderful and bright.
The chair is finally found among some junk,
with a weasel on it and a sneaky little skunk!